DISCARD

Energy And Action
GO AND STOP

John Marshall, Ed.D.

The Rourke Book Co., Inc.
Vero Beach, Florida 32964

PHOTO CREDITS
All photos © Barbara Patten

Library of Congress Cataloging-in-Publication Data

Marshall, John, 1944-
    Go and stop / John Marshall.
        p. cm. — (Energy and action)
    Includes index.
    ISBN 1-55916-152-3
    1. Force and energy—Juvenile literature. [1. Force and energy.
2. Gravity. 3. Friction.] I. Title. II. Series.
QC73.4.M383 1995
531'.6—dc20   95-10536
                                            CIP
                                            AC

Printed in the USA

TABLE OF CONTENTS

What Is Science? 5

Things That Go 6

Force 8

Force and Energy 11

A Crazy Science Mystery 12

What Is Gravity? 14

Let's Stop 17

Friction Helps Us Stop 18

The Force Is with You 20

Glossary 23

Index 24

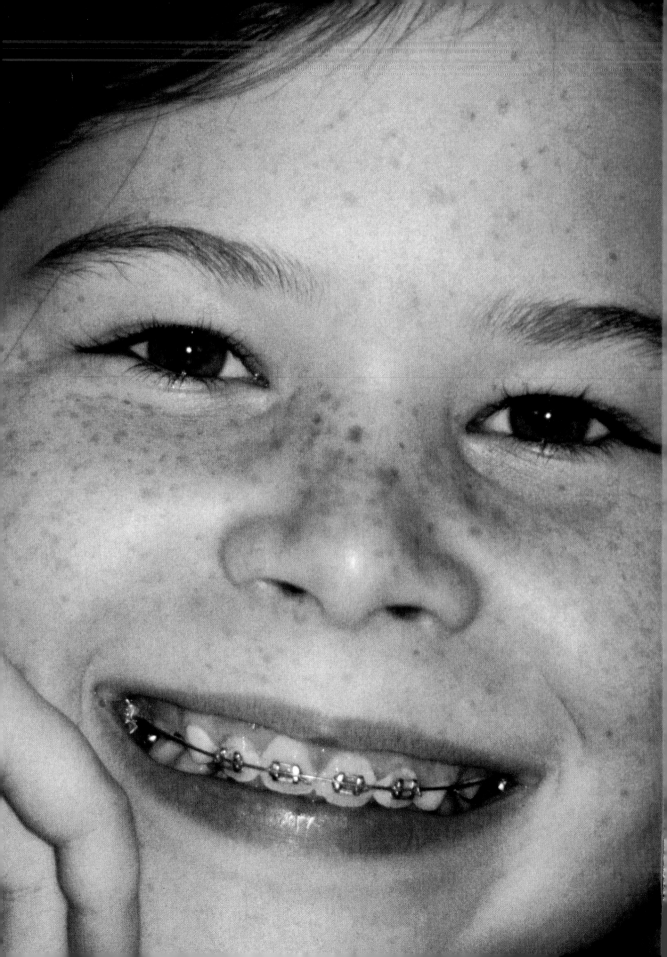

WHAT IS SCIENCE?

Push your sister on the swing.

Pull down the window shade.

Stop running in the hall!

We hear these words *push, pull* and *stop* every day. Have you ever wondered how things go and stop?

Children like you make good scientists because they wonder all the time and ask, "Why?" Let's read all about **force** (FORS), **gravity** (GRAV ih tee) and **friction** (FRIK shun).

You may be surprised what these three little words—push, pull and stop—mean to scientists.

Kids make great scientists because they
ask how and why.

THINGS THAT GO

The world is filled with moving things. Cars and trucks travel around town. Children run and jump. Horses gallop, bunnies hop and birds fly.

Now that's a lot of moving. Scientists know that nothing moves without some help.

This bird uses its wings and wind currents to move through the air.

Roller blades need force from you to move.

Things move when they are pushed or pulled. That's how they go. A push or pull that makes things move is called a force.

Your roller blades and bicycle will not move by themselves. They cannot take off down the sidewalk and zip around the corner. They need a force to make them go.

Where do you think the force comes from? Of course, it comes from you!

FORCE

You create force. You push and pull lots of things to make them move. You pull on your socks and push open the door. You even make yourself move by using force.

Some things only need a small force to make them move. With just a tiny pull on your pencil, your fingers pick it up.

However, moving a big bed across a room needs lots of force. It might take many people pushing and pulling to make a force big enough to move it—especially if you and your pet are on top.

Think about this. A bed is bigger than a pencil. It is made up of more **matter** (MAT er). Scientists say your bed has a greater **mass** (MASS), or amount of matter in it, than a pencil. It takes a big force to move a big mass.

Only a small force is needed to move this pencil.

8

FORCE AND ENERGY

It sure takes a lot of pushing and pulling to glide on roller blades or cruise on your bike. You swing your arms and move your legs to make the roller blades move. When you move your legs up and down, your bike goes. The more force you use, the faster you go.

Energy (EN er jee) is the power behind force. Our bodies make energy from the foods we eat. This energy gives us the power to use our muscles to push and pull.

Things like machines and automobiles go without people pushing or pulling. The force to make them go comes from energy made with electricity or gasoline.

This boy needs good food to supply his body with energy.

A CRAZY SCIENCE MYSTERY

You can have fun and find out a lot by pretending. Imagine you're a science detective brought in to solve a crazy mystery. Something very important is missing from the planet Earth. What is it?

These are your clues:

1. Cows are floating in the air.
2. People are walking on walls and ceilings.
3. Pizza is drifting around the lunch room.

Pretending is one way to figure out interesting things.

Gravity is the force that holds this laundry on the floor.

What on Earth has gone wrong? How could cows, people and pizza fly around without an airplane?

That's it! The force that holds cows on the ground, people on the floor and pizza on the table must not be working. Gravity, the Earth's natural pull on all objects, is missing.

WHAT IS GRAVITY?

Gravity is a natural force that pulls everything toward the center of the Earth. You cannot see gravity, but it is always around us.

If you jump in the air, you will not float away. Earth's gravity pulls you back down. If you lose your balance on your bike or roller blades, it's gravity that makes you fall.

Leaping frogs, bouncing balls, flying Frisbees and soaring kites that don't get tangled in trees must fall back to Earth. The force, or attraction, of gravity is always on duty, keeping your feet—and everything else—on the ground.

Gravity is trying to pull these books toward the Earth.

LET'S STOP

Now that we've found out about gravity, let's get back to roller blading and biking. Let's grab our safety helmets, look both ways and we're off to discover a different kind of force.

Hey, look out! The friendly old dog is sleeping in the middle of the sidewalk. He's not moving out of the way. Stop!

Wow! That was a close one. We're still on our feet, so we didn't use gravity to stop. How did we do it?

You dragged the heel on your roller blade against the sidewalk, or squeezed the brakes against the wheel rims on your bike. A special force called friction helped us stop.

Friction happens when the brake pads rub against the rim of the wheel.

FRICTION HELPS US STOP

Friction happens when two things rub together—like bike brakes against wheel rims. Friction makes things slow down and stop. When an object moves over a rough surface, it creates lots of friction. It's hard for the object to keep moving. Can you roller blade faster in tall grass or on a cement sidewalk? Very smooth objects can move faster and farther over very smooth surfaces.

Sandpaper rubbing on wood makes friction and heat.

Smooth tires don't make enough friction to safely stop cars.

At the bowling alley the lanes are smooth, just like the bowling balls. Only a small amount of friction is created when you roll the ball down the lane. You can roll the ball fast and knock lots of pins over.

Let's do a friction experiment on the slides at the playground. First, slide down on the seat of your pants. Now, climb back up the ladder and slide down on your bare knees. Ouch! What creates more friction—cloth against metal or skin against metal?

THE FORCE IS WITH YOU

Many forces are hard at work getting us going, keeping us from floating away, and helping us stop.

Energy is the power behind force. Our energy, the power behind all our pushing and pulling, is made from the healthy food we eat. Machine energy usually comes from electricity or gasoline.

Of course, the force of gravity holds us on the ground so we can roller blade and bike. Gravity is always tugging at everything, pulling toward the center of the Earth.

Friction, the force created when two objects rub together, helps us slow down and stop. Lucky for us and that old, sleepy dog, friction is always working, too.

Can you name all the forces at work here?

GLOSSARY

energy (EN er jee) — the power behind force

force (FORS) — the push and pull that makes things move

friction (FRIK shun) — the force created by two objects rubbing together

gravity (GRAV ih tee) — the force that pulls everything toward the center of the Earth

mass (MASS) — the amount of matter in an object

matter (MAT er) — what all living and nonliving things are made of

This old, sleepy dog is going to buy some healthy food for more energy.

INDEX

electricity   11, 20

energy   11, 20

force   5, 7, 8, 11, 13, 14, 17, 20

friction   5, 17, 18, 19, 20

gasoline   11, 20

gravity   5, 13, 14, 17, 20

mass   8

matter   8